Ancient Greece

A Concise Overview of the Greek History and Mythology Including Classical Greece, Hellenistic Greece, Roman Greece and The Byzantine Empire

Eric Brown

© Copyright 2018 by Eric Brown - All rights reserved.

The following eBook is produced with the goal of providing information that is as accurate and reliable as possible. Regardless, purchasing this eBook can be construed as consent to the fact that both the publisher and the author are in no way experts on the topics discussed within, and that any recommendations or suggestions that are made herein are for entertainment purposes only. Professionals should be consulted, as needed, prior to undertaking any of the action endorsed.

This declaration is deemed fair and valid by both the American Bar Association and the Committee of Publishers Association and is legally binding throughout the United States.

Furthermore, the transmission, duplication, or reproduction of any part of the following work, including specific information, will be considered an illegal act; irrespective of it being done electronically or in print. This extends to creating a secondary or tertiary copy of the work, or a recorded copy, and is only allowed with express written consent from the Publisher. All additional rights reserved.

The information in the following pages is broadly considered to be a truthful and accurate account of facts. As such, any inattention, use, or misuse of the information in question by the reader will render any resulting actions solely under his purview. There are no scenarios in which the publisher or the original author of this work can be deemed liable for any hardship or damage that may befall the reader after undertaking any information described herein.

Additionally, the contents of the following pages are intended only for informational purposes; thus, it should be thought of as universal. As befitting its nature, it is presented without assurance regarding its prolonged validity or interim quality. Trademarks that are mentioned are done without written consent and can in no way be considered an endorsement from the trademark holder.

Table of Contents

Chapter 1: Mycenaean Greece and the Late Bronze Age Collapse 8
The Ancient in Ancient Greece 8
Mycenaean Greece 9
Late Bronze Age Collapse... 11

Chapter 2: Archaic Greece 15
Cultural Developments 17
Military Developments... 26

Chapter 3: Classical Greece.. 28
The Fifth Century BC 29
The Fourth Century BC 36

Chapter 4: Hellenistic Greece 41
The Diadochi 45
The Rise of Rome 48

Chapter 5: Roman Greece 54
Early Roman History 55
The Early Roman Empire 57
Late Roman Empire 62

Chapter 6: The Byzantine Empire and the Greek Legacy 67
Invasions and Changing Times... 67
Disease... 69

Final Thoughts 71

Conclusion 72

Introduction

Congratulations on downloading Ancient Greece and thank you for doing so.

The following chapters will discuss the epic story of Ancient Greece throughout its varied and fascinating eras. We will begin our glorious journey of discovery in the very distant past that most of it is lost to the sands of time, and the stories that continue to live on do so mostly through myth and legend.

In chapter 1, we will travel back in time to Mycenaean Greece during the great Bronze Age. This epic period in civilization gave birth to bronze tools and weapons, and proto-writing. At its end, the Bronze Age saw a massive, global collapse that would claim the victory of most of the world's civilizations and plunge the entire world into the Dark Age. It is from the ashes of the Greek Dark Ages that Ancient Greece would rise.

In chapter 2, we begin our journey into the Greece of Classical Antiquity. Emerging first from this era was the Archaic period, which saw a dramatic increase in population and with it structural and social revolutions. More importantly, we will go through the crucial developments that transpired during this historic period.

On Classical Antiquity, chapter 3 elaborates on the vast history of Greece through its Classical Era. We will learn about the massive changes in Greek culture during this era that spanned a period of two centuries. This period marked a myriad of developments and progress in culture; the effects and principles of which we still see today.

Chapter 4 will then guide is through Ancient Greece's strong and proud Hellenistic period. This period saw the peak of Greek cultural influence and Alexander the Great conquest of nearly the entire known world. The Hellenistic period would then suffer decline and, ultimately, conquest by the Roman Empire – more in chapter 5 Interestingly, Greek culture continued to flourish during Roman reign.

Finally, in chapter 6, we will take a look at the events that transpired after the decline of Ancient Greece, most notably the rise and turbulent transition into the Byzantine Empire. We'll dig deep into the changing role that the old and noble civilization of Greece was to have down through history in its tumultuous path into the modern world.

There are plenty of books with this subject on the market, but we thank you for choosing this one! Every effort was made to ensure it is full of as much useful information as possible. Please enjoy!

Chapter 1: Mycenaean Greece and the Late Bronze Age Collapse

The entire epic and grand history of Ancient Greece was an ancient, long-lasting civilization that saw the birth of some of the most fundamental elements of our society today. These fundamental elements include many of the major core concepts of philosophy, the earliest and most enduring military tactics, and practices, as well as innovations in political thought that gave rise to democracy itself.

However, before we dive too deeply into the great coalition of ancient City-States known as Ancient Greece, it would be wise for us to take a brief look at the surrounding historical narrative that set the scene for its ascension. We'll a primer on much of the context and the pre-history of the region so we can get the deepest and firmest grasp on our topic as we possibly can.

The Ancient in Ancient Greece

A robust comprehension of the setting and historical context of Ancient Greece's eventual cultural innovations will mean going back to a basic understanding of Greek identity and how it was shaped by the preceding civilization. Also, we will look into the Dark Age that followed the culture's collapse. As a reference, we will be using the term "Classical Antiquity" to describe the period that was largely defined by the rise and decline of Ancient Greece. This period is in contrast to the previous period, which we broadly refer to as the Bronze Age.

The Bronze Age, of course, was not just a small blip in the great historical timeline. Rather, it was a grand period of human growth and cultural development. As it pertains to Greece, the Bronze Age is generally referred to as the Helladic period by archaeologists of the modern era. This name is derived from the name Hellas, which was the name by which these early proto-Greek peoples called themselves. These modern archaeologists then subdivide the Helladic period into three distinct sub-periods. These sub-periods are known as the Early Helladic period, the Middle Helladic period, and finally, the Late Helladic period.

Mycenaean Greece

To understand the peoples of Ancient Greece, we will especially need to take a closer look at the era of the Late Helladic period and the culture that dominated the area during that time. This very early civilization was known as Mycenaean Greece, which was the prototypical society that would eventually form the basis for Ancient Greece many, many years later.

When we look at the Late Helladic period of Mycenaean Greek history, we can further divide this period into three even smaller sub-periods. These three sub-periods are commonly referred to as LHI, LHII, and LHIII. Again, we are going to take a particular interest on the latest of these periods, the LHIII, and examine how the highs and lows of this era shaped the Greek world to come. The LHIII is generally characterized as an era of great expansion that was followed by a sharp decline and finally a collapse that ended the Mycenaean civilization, along with many of their contemporary neighbors.

Many of this period's major innovations, which covered fields as broad as engineering, military infrastructure, and architecture, were first introduced by the Mycenaean Greeks. This period was also a time of vast and complex global trade that was crucial to the Mycenaean economy and societal infrastructure. In addition to all of these massive leaps in progress, Mycenaean Greece was home to one of the world's earlier forms of written script, which is known today to modern historians and linguists as the Linear B system. This very early system of written record gave us our first look at the Greek language. These records that have been miraculously preserved over the millennia also gave us our first records of Greek religion that at this point already included many of the figures and deities that would live on in the Olympic Pantheon in later generations of Greeks and Romans.

The societal structure of the Mycenaean culture at this time was a number of palace-based city-states dominated by a societal class of warrior elites and was held in place by rigid economic, social, and political systems.

Late Bronze Age Collapse

The very end of the Late Helladic era saw the Mycenaean culture perish in an event known to history as the Late Bronze Age collapse. The effects of this sudden and violent catastrophe were felt throughout the entire Eastern Mediterranean region, upon which all of the earliest and most advanced civilizations of the time were built. What followed was a period when the art of record keeping was lost and would not be seen again for several hundred years. This kind of cultural regression is what is known in retrospect as a Dark Age wherein an entire period is covered in a figurative darkness and records or historical writings that may shed light on the events that transpired do not exist.

The Late Bronze Age collapse affected not only the Mycenaeans but also many of the other dominant civilizations in the complex socio-economic structure of the Late Bronze Age world. Many of the most populous and prosperous cities in all of the Eastern Mediterranean, and by extension, the entire known world of the time, were either destroyed or abandoned.

The exact reason for this collapse is unclear, but several theories have been put forward, including socio-economic unrest and upheaval, disruption to the complex network of trade routes, and popular uprisings. Perhaps the most intriguing, however, is the evidence of mysterious unknown invaders that contemporaries referred to as the 'Sea Peoples'.

It is unclear who exactly the Sea Peoples were, but several theories have been put forward. Some of these theories offer up relatively simple and mundane explanations, for example, some popular hypotheses suggest that the Sea Peoples may have been the Philistines, the Minoans, the inhabitants of the island of Crete, or any number of other island dwelling Mediterranean cultures. Perhaps even a grand coalition of a number of these societies and cultures. On the fringe side of things, many historians (often of questionable credentials) are firmly convinced that the Sea Peoples were invaders from the land of Atlantis. Atlantis of course being the almost certainly fictional society that Plato spoke of in one of his allegories. Realistically, though, the Sea Peoples could have been any number of Bronze Age societies in existence in and around the Mediterranean and the Fertile Crescent at the time.

In all likelihood, the collapse was probably a combination of all of these factors. In any case, the events of this period later became the basis for much of the literature and mythology of Ancient Greece, including the Trojan Epic. We may not know exactly who the Trojans were, or even if there was a literal city called Troy. And we can be fairly certain that the more fantastical and mythical elements of the tales are likely exaggeration or fabrications, we know that it was the tales from the Bronze Age, mythologized by generations of oral history, became much of the Greek and Roman mythology we know today.

In the Dark Age that followed this the Late Bronze Age Collapse, however, details are very scarce as to what was happening in the ancient world. The only one of the great civilizations to have survived the Late Bronze Age Collapse, although barely, and having suffered the loss of their written language and many other societal and technological advances, were the Egyptians, who interacted extensively with the Greeks at the time. But even the surviving records from the Egyptians, while confirming the invasions of the Sea Peoples and corroborating much of the evidence of social unrest and economic crisis during the era, they tell us very little about what the various peoples who survived the Dark Age did to survive, or what kind of lives they lived.

In any event, while the Late Bronze Age Collapse prevents us from having full knowledge of what our ancient ancestors did to survive a civilization-ending crisis, it does show us without any doubt that human beings certainly have the ability and the desire to survive. And the Mycenaeans, although devastated by profound and wide-ranging disaster did in fact survive. They survived, they adapted, they fought and eventually, they thrived. And these people, crawling out of the ashes of a doomed civilization, rose to become one of the greatest, most powerful and most culturally significant civilizations the world has ever seen.

This is the story of Ancient Greece.

Chapter 2: Archaic Greece

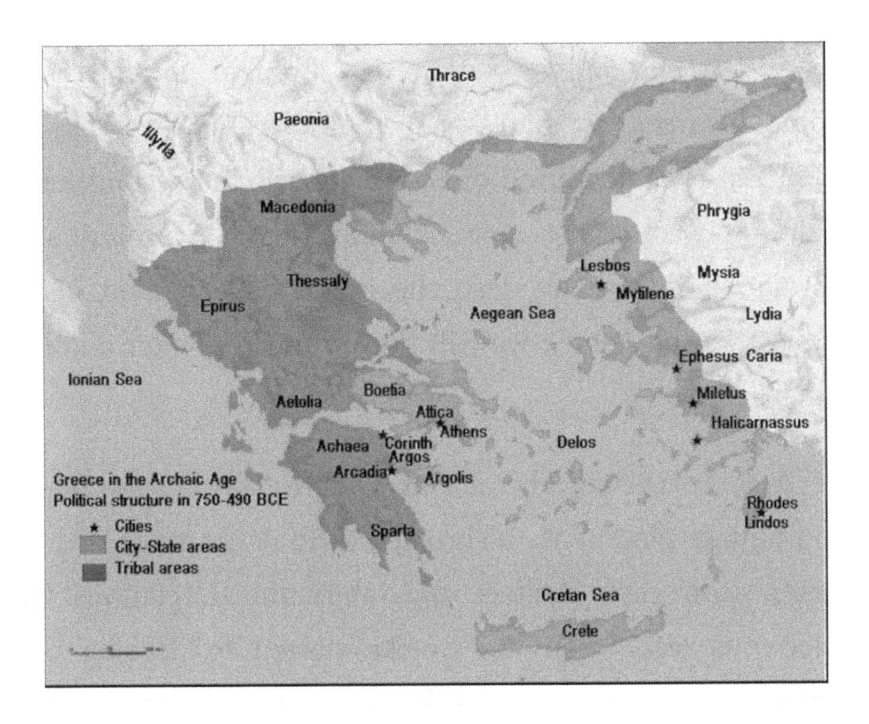

The world of the Ancient Mediterranean emerges from the period of Dark Ages firmly entrenched in what later became known as the Iron Age. For Greece, this brought about a period in its history that we today call Archaic Greece, and began immediately following the Greek Dark Ages in and around the eighth century BC. The beginning of this period was marked by sharp and large increases in the population of Greece. At the same time, a string of major social changes made the society Greece was becoming virtually unrecognizable to the Greece of the previous eras.

There were two major changes that became the basis for this period in Greek history. The first of these important changes was what has been termed the structural revolution which helped define the political map of the Ancient Greek world. This is the cultural revolution that brought to power the traditional Greek city-states such as Athens and Sparta. By the end of the Archaic period of Greek history, the second major revolution was taking place, the intellectual revolution. A reformation that would lead the major development of the Classical Period, which we will into in much greater detail in the next chapter.

The Archaic period of Ancient Greece saw a number of important development and broad growth in the areas of Greek culture, economics, politics, and international relations. The period was also when the Greeks started to develop their proclivity for warfare and developed the units and tactics that would lead them to military supremacy for centuries to come.

Also of major importance is the advent of the Greek alphabet which would lead to some of the other critical advances of this time. The earliest known Greek literature to have survived until modern times were composed in the Archaic period, along with many of the monuments and sculptures that directs our historians to this day.

The Archaic period of Greece is generally considered to have started at the time of the foundation of the Olympic Games. It took place in 776 BC and marks a major historical and cultural turning point. For a long time, the Greek Archaic period was considered to be of less historical importance than the later Classical and Hellenistic periods, but these attitudes have more recently changed. The Archaic periods is seen by experts with a renewed sense of importance.

One of the primary sources we have for information in this period is from the Greek writer Herodotus, usually called the first historian. While Herodotus often omits dates, and many of his writings could rightly be considered mythology. Nevertheless, his accounts make up the basis of much of our knowledge.

Cultural Developments

The Archaic period of Ancient Greece was a time of major cultural development and social change. One of the biggest shifts of the period was the changes in the political landscape of the Greek world. Prior to this time, most settlements and cities were under the control of warlords and were essentially tribal bands with early, proto-democratic systems. In the Archaic period, Greece witnessed the development of the polis or city-state, as what we know today. During this time, the polis became the central point of political organization. While we tend to think of Ancient Greece as a type of nation or empire, this concept is not entirely correct. Ancient Greece should be more accurately thought of as a loose coalition of city-states that were culturally tied together by a common language.

Each of these city-states was self-organized and self-governed. Many of the individual city-states that made up Greece were ruled by leaders. Collectively, they are to be known as the tyrants. These tyrants governed with an early form of autocratic rule. At the same time, however, this period of Greek history also has come to show some of the earliest evidence for the development of constitutional structures and law codes, both of which indicate the birth of an early law system, as well of a form of community-based decision-making. By the end of the Archaic period of Ancient Greece, the two most dominant cities, Sparta and Athens, seem to have developed their respective constitutions. These constitutions' forms were maintained and would be considered their classical forms.

In eighth and seventh centuries BC, the people of the Greek cities began to spread out. Citizens settle throughout the Mediterranean, the Black Sea, and the Sea of Marmara. While much of this travel was done for the purpose of establishing and maintaining trade routes and contacts, these travels were also made in the interest of settling and securing new territory. These new settlements grew to become independent city-states of their own. The independent city-states are one of the primary distinguishing characteristics of Ancient Greece. It is important to note that the new settlements would be unlike the case under an empirical system, such as Rome or the British Empire of many centuries later.

There were two different and distinct ways in which the Ancient Greeks settled new territory outside of Greece. The first was the way in which a detachment of Greeks would found a city which would serve as an independent *polis*. The other form of Ancient Greek settlement in this period was what modern historians refer to as an emporium, or in the plural form *emporia*. These were essentially trading posts which were colonized and inhabited by Greeks and non-Greeks alike. The primary purpose of these emporia was to manufacture goods for sale and export.

Some of the first Greek colonies to have been founded at this time were located on the island known as Sicily. These early colonies were founded by people from various different city-states all around throughout Greece. By the waning years of the eighth century BC, there had also been a number of well-established Greek settlements throughout the southern regions of modern day Italy.

During the seventh century BC, the Greek colonists continued to expand throughout the areas in which they had settled and become established. In the more western reaches of the Greek culture, settlements were established as far away from the nucleus of Greek society as modern day Marseilles. On the eastern side of this cultural explosion, the Greek cultural spread reached well into the north of the Aegean, as well as throughout the Black Sea and the Sea of Marmara. Securing new territory and generating new colonists became a major part of the game of political dominance in this era of Greek history

Toward the end of the Archaic era, the Southern region of modern-day Italy and the entirety of what is Sicily today had received a massive influx of Greek colonizers. At this point, there had been so many Greek settlements founded within the reaches of southern Italy and Sicily that it had come to be called as Magna Graecia or Great Greece. Records indicate that land was being settled in the region at a rate of no less than one settlement for every other year. The pattern of rapid settlement continued throughout modern-day Italy well into the middle of the fifth century BC.

While this period was certainly a time of rapid growth and development, there was a darker side to the cultural spread. Today, the period of Archaic Greece is sometimes referred to as the Age of Tyrants. The Ancient Greek word *tyrannos*, from which we derive the modern word tyrant, was first seen in contemporary Greek literature of the time in a poem written by Archilochus. Tyrannos was used to describe Gyges, a Lydian ruler. The earliest Greek ruler who fits the description of a tyrant was the leader Cypselus, who took power by force in a coup during the year 655 BC. This was followed by a veritable trend of tyranny throughout the Archaic Greek word during the middle of the seventh century BC.

Many different explanations have been put forward to explain for the socio-political shift to tyranny as a ruling standard. One particularly notable example goes all the way back to the writings and teachings of Aristotle. He felt that tyranny was a natural side effect of the ruling class becomes more and more intolerable. He argued that tyrants were actually chosen and installed by the people as a reaction to a deeply unpopular ruling class. More modern approaches explain that the tyranny phenomenon has focused more on identifying powerful men that controlled large, private armies. They utilized intimidation to seize power. Other theories, suggests that it was oligarchs fighting among themselves that lead to tyranny, rather than the power struggles between these powerful oligarchs and the people.

It is important to note that the population of Greece doubled during the eighth century BC. The growth in population resulted in more settlements being founded further afield. These new settlements were even larger than they had been previously.

The population boom was not isolated to Greece. The upturn was actually part of a broader phenomenon of growth in population that was happening all across the Mediterranean area during this time. As we are more aware, large-scale population shifts and human activities of this nature can have a massive effect on the natural climate and environment. It is believed that the population growth that happened across the Mediterranean region during this period directly resulted in a notable climatic shift that occurred between the years of 850 BC and 750 BC. The climate of the region became much cooler and wetter than normal.

While this was certainly a period of rapid development and of intense land-seizure, there was still a fair amount of arable land that was not yet being used for cultivation in Greece in the Archaic period. Despite the fact that much land was available, and ever increasing as new settlements were founded, it seems that farms in this period were primarily concentrated very close to the established settlements. Farms were small, cohesive units.

Evidence shows that crop rotation practices had been well established by this point. It was particularly common to alternate between cereals and legumes. Farmers also allowed the land to be left fallow on alternating years to maintain ground nutrients.

The crops were also highly diversified and farmers tended to grow a large variety of crops simultaneously. This practice allowed for the more consistent use of human resources all throughout the year. The strategy also provided a degree of protection against crop failure, as it was highly unlikely for all of the various crops to fail during one season.

Apart from this manner of subsistence farming, the Ancient Greeks also cultivated a wide variety of luxury items and cash crops which they would sell both locally and abroad for great profit. Such cash crops included olives and vines, as well as various fruits and vegetable.

Livestock played an important role in the agriculture and economy but it was notably of secondary importance. Some domesticated animals, particularly goats and sheep, were kept for wool, milk, meat, and fertilizer. Livestock was very difficult to maintain. Average farmers may have kept a few animals for meat or milk, but large herds were prohibitively expensive to maintain. Owning a large herd is generally a sign of extreme wealth. For instance, a team of oxen would have gone a long way to significantly improve agricultural yields but it would be too expensive for the average farmer. Only the affluent would have been able to afford horses or particularly large herds of cattle.

Trade was absolutely fundamental to the economy and

infrastructure of not only Greece but the entire Mediterranean region and the Aegean Sea by the later years of the eighth century BC. The advanced and extensive trade network led to a large degree of cultural exchange in the early days of Archaic Greece. An evidence is a strong oriental influence on Greek art.

As many of the Greek colonies throughout Southern Italy and Sicily became larger and more powerful, trade continued between them. The older, earlier Greek settlements throughout the Mediterranean. This led to a strengthening of cultural unity throughout the entire region and began to solidify Greece as a cultural and economic powerhouse.

The Greek islands as we know them today, where the central hub for eastern trade. It acted as an intermediary between mainland Greece and the lands of the east. Throughout this period and into the sixth century BC, the eastern Greek city-states became very, very prosperous on account of vast and robust trade routes with Egypt and Asia. Corinth, along with the other more coastal city-states of the Greek mainland, received the largest portions of the trade from the east.

Greek art from the various city-states also became a major element in trade during this period. It resulted in both the production and development of Greek art, along with serving to bolster Greek trade even further.

Visual arts during the Archaic period of Ancient Greece also underwent significant changes in style and craft. Many pieces of art have been preserved from this time. They can generally be characterized by more naturalistic and representational styles. Monumental sculpture was first introduced in the Greek world during this time. The art of pottery went through massive stylistic shifts. Both pottery and sculpture were both heavily influenced by oriental styles. The Archaic period of history in Ancient Greece also saw some major innovations in literature, notably including the advent and development of the Greek alphabet. We also have evidence that the earliest surviving Greek poetry was composed during this period.

When the Greek Dark Ages preceded the Ancient and Archaic periods of Greek history, the art and science of writing were lost in Greece. It is highly probable that by the ninth century BC, no one left in Greece would have been able to understand the Bronze Age Linear B system of writing. However, after the ninth century BC, there is evidence of objects being imported into the Greek that was inscribed with Phoenician writing. This Phoenician script formed the basis for what would eventually become the Greek Alphabet. Developed during the eighth century BC. By the middle years of the eighth century BC, pottery with Greek inscriptions begin to become evident.

These early inscriptions in the Greek alphabet generally tend to be for the purpose of identifying or explaining the object where it is inscribed.

Military Developments

During the Archaic period, the military experienced what many would consider one of the most historically important developments in the world. The development was the adoption of the Hoplite in warfare by the Greek city-states. This major adoption occurred during the earlier years of the seventh century BC. The Hoplite armor, called the panoply, appeared as early as the eighth century BC. The city-state of Argos was the location of the discovery of the earliest known examples of the panoply armor in the eighth century BC.

The panoply was composed of several different individual pieces of armor. Although individual pieces of arms and armor had been used and developed for centuries, the complete panoply cannot be proven to have been in use until about 675 BC. A Corinthian vase painting dated to this year has been found depicting a soldier equipped in the entire panoply.

In fact, the word panoply can be translated to something similar to "all arms" in modern English. The panoply itself refers to the entire set of all of the pieces of armor that compose the full set of armor for the Hoplite. It equates to a heavy-armed soldier or heavy infantry. The complete panoply would include a helmet, breastplate, and greaves, along with a sword and shield and a lance. Contrary to popular belief, the primary weapon of the Hoplite was the lance, or spear, not the sword. The sword was mostly used as a backup or emergency weapon, only after the Hoplite's main weapon, the spear, was lost or broken.

Another military innovation that cannot be understated is the development and adoption of phalanx tactics in combat. This method of unit formation was used by Hoplite unities all throughout the Classical period of Ancient Greece. The first evidence that was have uncovered that shows this tactical method in use does not occur until around the middle of the seventh century BC.

In the world of naval military development, the trireme was first developed and implemented during the Archaic period. Up until the eighth century BC, ships warships that employed two banks of oars and oarsmen had commonly been used by Greek navies. By the seventh century BC, the three-banked trireme had become more popular and commonplace. In the middle of the seventh century BC, Corinth likely became the first place in Greece to adopt the trireme, but it wasn't until a hundred years later that it became the most popular battleship design.

Chapter 3: Classical Greece

The period of time that we now refer to as the Classical Greece period was the era in Greek culture that spanned for in and around two hundred years between the fifth and fourth centuries BC. During this very historically important and significant period of time, Ancient Greece suffered the annexation of much of the territory that is currently sovereign to modern-day Greece by the great Persian Empire. After a period of foreign occupation, this same territory later became independent once more. This era of Classical Greece became a massive and strong influence on the Roman Empire. The Roman Empire would soon begin to rise as well as the large majority of western civilization all the way through subsequent history even up until this very day.

Modern politics in the west, with the artistic thought such as architecture and sculpture, philosophy, literature, theatre, and scientific concepts are derived and defined by the culture, developments, and ideologies of this period of time in Ancient Greece.

The most commonly cited events used as time markers for which to define the Classical period of Ancient Greece begin with the fall of the final tyrant in Athens in the year 510 BC and end with the death of Alexander the Great in the year 323 BC. This corresponds roughly to the fifth and fourth centuries BC. In the context of the culture, art, and architecture of Ancient Greece, these two centuries define the Classical period. Therefore by this reckoning, the Classical period of Ancient Greece comes immediately after the Archaic period and the Hellenistic period.

The Fifth Century BC

Beginning in the fifth century BC, in other words, the earliest years of Classical Greece culture, until approximately the end of the fifth century BC, which would correspond roughly to the mid-point of the Classical period, much of the academic study pertaining to Ancient Greece is examined through the lens of the Athenians. Athens of this time period has provided us the most plays, narratives, and other written documents, records and works of any of the Ancient Greek city-states.

The period that our modern times refer to as the fifth century BC extends, a small amount, into the fourth century BC because the calendar of the time was vastly different than that of ours today. By looking at it from this point of view, we could consider the first major event of that century to be the Cleisthenes' reforms. These events occurred following the fall of the last tyrant in Athens, during the year 508 BC. However, from a wider perspective of the entire Greek world of its Classical era, it could be argued that the beginning could be the Ionian Revolt with took place in the year 500 BC. This is the event that caused the first Persian invasion which happened in 492 BC. Persians would come to dominate much of the political and military worlds of Ancient Greece during the entire Classical era.

At the very beginning of the Classical era of Ancient Greece, Spartan soldiers assisted the Athenians in overthrowing their king, the tyrant known as Hippias, son of Peisistratos. The king of Sparta at the time, Cleomenes I, installed a pro-Spartan oligarchy in the city-state lead by Isagoras. However, Cleomenes I had a rival, Cleisthenes. Cleisthenes secured the support from the middle class and at the same time was helped by Democrats. With this strategic support and assistance, Cleisthenes was able to take control of the city. Cleomenes I tried to prevent the takeover from occurring at various periods in between the year 508 BC and the year 506 BC, but he was not able to prevent Cleisthenes from keeping control as he gained the full support of the Athenians.

The changes during this time came to be known as the Cleisthenes' reforms. Through these reforms, the people of Athens were able to endow their city with isotonic institutions. Isotonic institutions in this context refer to equal rights for citizens. Equal rights for all citizens were indeed implemented under the Cleisthenes' reforms, although it is important to note that these reforms were not truly an equally representative society, as only men were free citizens. The reforms set in place by Cleisthenes also established ostracism as a form of punishment and deterrence for the people of Athens. Ostracism was a custom and practice through which an Athenian citizen could be exiled for ten years from the city-state of Athens. It was often used as a pre-emptive measure to prevent a citizen who may have been perceived as being overly ambitious from rising to become a future tyrant.

While Greece was a major cultural, economic and geopolitical power during the Classical period, it was by certainly not the only powerful political entity on the world stage. To their east, gradually gaining power and dominance, was the Persian Empire. Even by the middle of the sixth century BC, the Persian Empire had begun to exert its control over neighboring Greece. The city-states in the region of Ionia, now located at the Aegean coast of modern Turkey, were unable to remain independent under the pressure of the encroaching Persian Empire and eventually came under their rule.

Eventually, in the year 499 BC, the Greek population of the Ionian region rose up against their Persian occupiers in what became known as the Ionian Revolt. A few other Greek city-states sent assistance to the cause. These events began the Battle of Lade in the year 494 BC. The Greeks were defeated and forced out of Ionia. After this significant Greek defeat, the entire region of Ancient Asia Minor returned to the control of the Persian Empire.

By the end of the first decade of the fifth century BC, the Persian Empire had subjugated Thrace and conquered Macedonia. A successful naval campaign in the Aegean Sea was also led at this time.

In the year 490 BC, the man who would eventually become quite possibly the most famous of the Persian Emperors, Darius the Great, sent a fleet of Persian warships to punish the Greeks. Darius the Great's army intended to take Athens by landing in Attica, but in the battle that ensued, the Battle of Marathon, the Persian army was soundly defeated by the general Miltiades of Athens. The Greek army had 1,000 Plataeans and 9,000 Athenian hoplites. The survivors of the Persian fleet moved on to Athens. Since Athens was strongly garrisoned, the Persians chose to call of any attempt at an assault.

Darius the Great was succeeded by Xerxes I. In the year 480 BC, the new king sent a much stronger force of some three hundred thousand soldiers by land with the support of 1,207 battleships across the Hellespont by means of a double pontoon bridge. The Persian army took over Thrace and then continued on to Thessaly and Boeotia, while the Persian navy ran interference and attempted to blockade the waterway.

King Leonidas I, the king of Sparta during the Agiad Dynasty, was able to delay the Persian army at the famous Battle of Thermopylae. In this legendary battle, three hundred Spartan soldiers went up against the entire Persian army. However, despite fighting bravely and giving their lives to slow down Xerxes I and his army, the Persians were still able to advance on Attica. Soon after, they captured and set fire to Athens, razing it to the ground. The majority of mainland Greece, just about every city-state north of the Isthmus of Corinth, had fallen to Persian control. Favorably, prior to the Battle of Thermopylae, the Athenians had been wisely evacuated from the city by means of the sea. Commanded by the great general Themistocles, Athens was able to secure a major turning point in the war with the defeat the Persian fleet at the Battle of Salamis.

By the year 483 BC, Greece was right in the middle of a time of peace in between the two Persian invasions. During this time, in a small, rural area in the vicinity of the city-state of Athens, a rich vein of silver ore was discovered. The vast wealth from this discovery was used in order to build some two hundred battleships that would be used to combat piracy in the Aegean Sea. The next year, under the command of the Spartans, the Greeks were able to defeat the Persian army. The Persian forces retreat from Greece and they would never again attempt another invasion.

Shortly after the Persian Invasions, Athens put it upon itself to unify the Greek city-states into an alliance that came to be called the Delian League. Sparta did not participate in this alliance and went into isolation. Athens became the most powerful commercial and naval power among the Classical Greek city-states.

During the latter half of the fifth century BC, the Classical Greek world had essentially split into two rival leagues or coalitions of Greek city-states. The first and ostensibly most powerful was the Delian League which centered on Athens. The rival league of Greek city-states began to arise which was centered on Sparta. As the threat from their neighbors in the Persian Empire began to subside, this coalition became more and more important. This Spartan league in known now as the Peloponnesian League.

There had been city-state coalitions in Greece in the past, including the Hellenic League, and well as the contemporary Delian League. These previously established coalitions had been formed in response to some form of external threat. The Peloponnesian League, on the other hand, existed for the sole and explicit purpose of putting strength and muscle behind Spartan policy. Its intention is to exert dominance and influence over the entire Peloponnese (a region in southern

Greece) Peninsula. As these two internal powers jockeyed for dominance, the relations between them eventually deteriorated to the point of the war. This war is known today as the Peloponnesian War.

The initial strategy of Sparta in the opening stages of the Peloponnesian war was to take Attica by invasion. However, the Athenians managed to retreat and take shelter behind their walls. They were safe from the Spartan invaders behind their walls but an unexpected enemy reared its head in the form of a plague. The outbreak killed many people including the great general and orator, Pericles. After a few years of inconclusive fighting, a temporary peace was declared.

Hostilities were resumed, however, some years later, in the year 418 BC, after a conflict between Argos, an ally of Athens, and Sparta led to another full-scale war. After several more years of conflict all throughout the Ancient Greek world, the Peloponnesian War finally began to wind down at the end of the fifth century BC. Athens eventually was faced with bankruptcy after losing her entire fleet. The Spartans, on the other hand, received assistance from Persian. Athens demanded peace and despite the harsh settlement demands from Sparta, peace was declared.

The Fourth Century BC

As we roll into the fourth century BC in Classical Greece, we see the Peloponnesian War had left Sparta as the undisputed master of Greece. However, the Spartan mentality and culture of warrior elitism did not lend well to this particular role. After only a short number of years, the Democratic Party had already begun to regain power within Athens and in other city-states throughout Ancient Greece. By the year 395 BC rulers in Sparta had removed their naval commander from office, and the naval supremacy was now lost. Again, Sparta's superiority was challenged by Athens, Thebes, Argos, and Corinth, though these last two were former allies to Sparta, in what came to be known as the Corinthian War. The war ended in the year 387 BC without no decisive victor. Before long though, the powers were gathering against Sparta once more. Sparta chose to end the Treaty of Antalcidas with Persia. The unexpected decision to end this treaty, as part of the agreement therein, involved Sparta turning over Ionia and Cyprus back to Persia not considering the centuries of Greek combat against Persia on behalf of those cities. This decision led to more city-states uniting against Sparta.

The Peloponnesian War turned out to be a major turning point in the world of Ancient Greece. Over the next few decades, Greece descended into a complex series of power grabs. All of the major players vied for dominance. All attempted to establish their respective city-state into an empire in its own right. The Spartans, the Athenians, the Thebans, and the Macedonians all make attempts at Greek dominance during the entire fourth century BC.

The first of these city-states to establish itself as a legitimate city-state-empire was Sparta. While they were able to exert a powerful dominance in the Classical Greek world, their dominance ended up being rather short-lived. Spartan military strength dropped steeply during their brief stint as an empire. In the end, they were unable to defend their own city from other city-states. By the year 378 BC, the city-state of Thebes had begun rather tired of Spartan control over them, and a popular uprising was instigated, and in the year 375 BC, the army of Thebes won a great victory over the Spartans, who had vastly superior numbers, at the Battle of Tegyra.

During this time, the military strength and authority of Thebes had grown so intensely in such a notably short amount of time, that Athens began to distrust the expand power Thebes was coming to have. Athens made the move to consolidate as much of her power as possible by forming the Athenian League for the second time. This growing powder keg finally exploded in the year 371 BC, when the Theban army and the Spartans Clashed in the Battle of Leuctra. The Thebes handed Sparta a decisive defeat. Sparta left the battlefield having lost a huge portion of its forces as well as four hundred of its two thousand citizen troops. This was a major turning point in the entire Greek history. The Theban victory at the Battle of Leuctra ended a very long stretch of extreme prestige and elitism of the Spartan military. Both the dominance of Sparta and its time hegemony had come to an end.

But despite Thebes being the victory in this watershed battle against Sparta, Thebes did not in fact gain hegemony in Classical Greece, but on the other hand, it was Athens that ended up securing hegemony and becoming dominant once again.

This then led to the period of time in which the second Athenian league became something of an Empire itself, exerting its hegemony over the other city-states of Greece. However, this new Athenian League didn't last very long either. In many ways, the second Athenian League only really existed to guard against Sparta. But now, with the fall of Sparta in the year 371 BC, the alliance lost its purpose for existing and fell to structural weakness. Without conflict with Sparta to fuel their Alliance, they lacked the means to achieve their most modest ambitions, let alone the lofty ones. They had a very difficult time to even finance their navy, without even taking into account the forces of their entire alliance, and as such, they were simply unable to defend themselves and their allies and were not able to stand up to any pressure from city-states outside the alliance.

From the year 360 BC onward, Athens began to lose what reputation it had, as the alliance began to fall apart and allied city-states began to secede from the alliance.

By the year 357 BC, this revolt against the Athenian League had spread, and Athens would be forced to go to war against its own allies. Eventually, as the tensions and conflict escalated, the neighboring Persian emperor intervened in the war on behalf of the city-states in revolt. The Persian Emperor made the demand of the Athenians that they recognize the independence of their allies. This ultimatum was served with a threat of invasion with two hundred triremes sailing against Athens if they did not comply. Athens was forced to leave both the war and the Confederacy, which only served to weaken the flagging city-state, and signaled the conclusion of Athenian hegemony in Classical Greece.

After another brief empiric rise and rule with Thebes taking a shot at hegemony, until the entire Greek world became eclipsed by Macedon, a major power on the rise, in the year 346 BC. With the rise of Macedon came the rise of one of the greatest and most enduring historical figures of all time, Alexander the Great.

Alexander the Great is a topic all to himself, and many books have been dedicated to him through the hundreds of years since his death, but needless to say, Alexander the Great's influence over Classic Greece was unprecedented and total. His father, Phillip the Second of Macedon, had the grand ambition of conquering the entire Greek world, although he died by an assassin's blade before he could see this ambition through. Alexander, however, took up his father's ambition and succeeded decisively.

Despite Alexander the Great's historical pedigree, however, his untimely death in the year 323 BC, at the age of just thirty-two, sent the Greek world back into chaos and fragmentation. With that, the Classical Greek period comes to an end.

Chapter 4: Hellenistic Greece

The Hellenistic period of Ancient Greek history roughly incorporates the time between when Alexander the Great died and concluded with the rise of the Roman Empire. In Ancient Greek, the word Hellas was the original name of Greece, and this is where the word Hellenistic can draw its lineage from.

This period is when the cultural influence of Greece as well as its power was at its zenith throughout the Mediterranean, as well as the rest of Europe, Western Asia, and Northern Africa. Considered as the golden age for Greece, the arts were flourishing along with theatre, literature, sciences, philosophy, mathematics, music, architecture, exploration, and all manner of other fields and disciplines. The Hellenistic period of Ancient Greek history is also considered to be one of acute transition and has even been associated with a time of degeneration and decadence, especially when compared to the relative period of enlightenment that was experienced during the Greek Classical period.

Many new and long-lasting cultural innovations were taking place during this period, including but certainly not limited to the rise of Alexandrian poetry, which is characterized by the influences from the Alexander the Great founded city of Alexandria. Also coming to prominence during this era was the concept of New Comedy, which developed all through the period of Macedonian rule. The Septuagint was written in this time, which is the earlier known Greek translation of the Hebrew Old Testament from the original language of Hebrew. Philosophy also saw a major renewal in development, with the emergence of both the Stoic and Epicurean school of philosophy, which both came into prominence during the Hellenistic period of Ancient Greece.

In the period, science in Greece was being advanced by the timeless, enduring works of the great mathematician Euclid. Important mathematical and scientific contributions were also developed by the no less talented and legendary polymath Archimedes.

The sphere of influence of the religious beliefs in Hellenistic Greece expanded and came to include new gods into their panthea, such as the Greco-Egyptian god Serapis or various eastern gods like Attis or Cybele. There was also a fair amount of cultural and religious exchange between Hellenistic culture and the Buddhism that was taking hold in Bactria as well as in the northwest of India at the time.

After the invasion and conquest of the Persian Empire by Alexander the Great in the year 330 BC, the Hellenistic kingdoms had been established all the way through the southwest areas of Asia. Included are the Seleucid Empire and the Kingdom of Pergamon, as well the north-east of Africa, where the Ptolemaic Kingdom was located, and finally South Asia, the area that included the Greco-Bactrian Kingdom and the Indo-Greek Kingdom. Alexander the Great's rise, conquest, and demise had certainly made major and long-lasting changes to the makeup and composure of the Greek world. The effect spread into the Hellenistic period of Ancient Greece and continue to influence the Greek world as well as the world at large for centuries to come.

The power vacuum caused by Alexander the Great's unexpected death was settled by dividing the empire into several far-flung kingdoms. The Hellenistic period of Greece was a fresh wave of Greek settlers spreading and colonizing. New Greek kingdoms were established in far-off city-states in the areas of Africa and Asia. Naturally, the vast spread of Greek people came with it widespread export of Greek culture and language, the results of which persisted up until our very modern day. In return, the far-flung new realms of Greek influence also took into themselves a very large amount of influence from the people indigenous to the area.

This pattern of varying and diverse cultural exchange is the reason for strong Greek cultural influence. Hellenistic culture came to represent the Ancient Greek world fusing with the cultures of the Middle East, Southwest Asia, and the Near East. It became very common for a Greek city-state, kingdom or realm to adopt customs and practices into their own culture, whether for practical purposes, strategic purposes, or otherwise, and thus the broader Greek world became something of a cultural melting pot at this period in time. This cultural and linguistic mixing also served to establish and spread new dialects of the Ancient Greek language. An example would be the Attic-based dialect that came to be known as Koine Greek, which is also known as Biblical Greek. It became the dominant trade language of the entire Hellenistic world.

There is no clear consensus among historians and Greek scholars as to what particular date or event marks the conclusion of the Hellenistic era of Ancient Greece. Several events have been put forward or have historically thought as the ending point of the Hellenistic world. The first such event would be the final and complete conquest of the primary heartlands of Greece by the Romans, which took place after the Achaean War in the year 146 BC. Another date proposed as an appropriate for the Hellenistic era of Greece is the final defeat and end of the Ptolemaic line of Kings, which occurred following the Battle of Actium in the year 31 BC. While other historians have even gone so far as to put forward that the Hellenistic era of Ancient Greece lasted all the up until the famous moving of the capital city of the Roman Empire from Rome to Constantinople by the Roman emperor Constantine the Great which happens centuries later in the year 330 AD.

The Diadochi

On June the 10th of the year 323 BC, Alexander the Great died, young and unexpectedly. Upon his untimely death, he left behind a massive empire which had been made up of the vast swaths of lands, territories, cities, and city-states that had been conquered during the famous and unprecedented campaigns of Alexander the Great. To govern and maintain such a vast empire, many of these territories and lands were made to be autonomous, self-governed regions which were known as satrapies. However, at the time of the death of Alexander the Great, he had not selected a successor to take up his rulership, the entire empire immediately plunged into a dispute between his generals to determine who should be the next king.

The wars of succession that came out of this chaotic state of affairs became known as the Diadochi wars, the first one which broke out shortly after the death of Alexander the Great. Ultimately there were three wars of the Diadochi that saw conflict all throughout the Eastern Mediterranean, Northern Africa, and as the Far East and modern-day Northern India. By the end of the wars of the Diadochi, the power balance that would be maintained for much of the Hellenistic Period of Ancient Greece was in place. There were three territorial division that made up the primary power structure of the Hellenistic age, with the first being Macedon, which at this time was under the control of Antigonus II Gonatas. The second was the Ptolemaic kingdom in Egypt which was under the rule of Ptolemy I, who had advanced quite considerably in age at this point in history. And finally, the third major power in of the Hellenistic age of Greece was the Seleucid Empire, which at this point in time was now ruled by the son of its founder Seleucus, Antiochus I Soter.

These wars of the Diadochi lasted until the end of the third war in the year 275 BC. The wars saw the fall of two once influential Macedonian dynasties, the Antipatrid and the Argead dynasties, which the Antigonus dynasty taking power in their stead. This era in the history of Greece and Macedonia also is notable for the successive wars that took place between the one-time allies of Macedon, the Aetolian League and the Achaean League, and the Kingdom of Macedonia itself.

Between the years of 221 BC and 179 BC, which was during the rulership of King Philip V of Macedon, the empire of Macedonia suffered significant military and political setbacks. First of all, they were defeated in the Cretan War, which took place between the years of 205 BC and 200 BC, by the forces of Rhodesia and its allies. And then secondly, the alliance with Carthage that was set out in the Macedonia-Carthaginian Treaty of the year 216 BC, drew Macedonia into a conflict with early Ancient Rome, a power on the rise, in what become known as the First Macedonian War, which took place between the years of 214 BC and 205 BC. Soon after which was followed by the Second Macedonia War, which took place not long after the first one, between the years of 200 BC and 197 BC.

In the aftermath of these wars and conflicts, Macedonia came to be perceived as being weak and vulnerable. This negative perception led the Seleucid Empire under the rule of Antiochus III the Great to invade mainland Greece, however, this decision would eventually backfire on Antiochus III the Great, and set off a chain reaction of events that eventually put Rome in a position of military dominance in the entire area.

It is important to note that during the Hellenistic period of Ancient Greece, the importance of the region properly known as Greece, and the historic Greek city-states declined considerably amongst the entire Greek-speaking world. During this time, the major centers of culture in the Hellenistic period and region where the cities of Antioch and Alexandria, which were the capitals of the Syrian Seleucid Empire and Ptolemaic Egypt, respectively. However, many other cities became important hubs of culture, art, ideas and so forth, and indeed, the increasing urbanization of the entire Hellenistic region of the Eastern Mediterranean was a particularly notably facet of this time period in history.

The Rise of Rome

In the year 192 BC, tensions between the rapidly developing Rome and the ruler of the Seleucid Empire, Antiochus III, boiled over into full-scale war. At this time, Greece was invaded by Antiochus III with a force of someone in the neighborhood of ten thousand men. He was also elected to the position of the commander in chief of the alliance led by the Aetolians. To the cities and city-states in the Greek world, it was unclear which side of this conflict had their best interest in mind, but many of them felt that Antiochus III would be their savior and protect them from Roman occupation and oppression. Macedon, however, decided that it would lend its support to Rome, as they felt that Rome was the way of the future.

In the year 191 BC, the Roman general Marius Acilius Glabrio forced Antiochus III to withdraw from Greece and into Asia, after the Roman forces routed Antiochus at Thermopylae (not to be confused with the Battle of Thermopylae some three hundred years earlier in which three hundred Spartan led by King Leonidas held back the entire invading Persian army at the Hot Gates, during the Classical period of Ancient Greece). It was during this military engagement that the Roman army moved for the first time into Asia, pursuing Antiochus III and defeating him once again in the year 190 BC, in the battle of Magnesia at Magnesia ad Sipylum.

By this time, the Greek world was right in the middle of Rome proper, and the territories that Rome was invading and conquering. This meant that during this period, the Roman army was a constant and more or less permanent fixture in the Greek world. In the year 188 BC, the Peace of Apamaea was declared, which put Rome in a position of unrivaled dominance throughout Greece.

Throughout the following years, as Rome became more and more entrenched in their role, they were drawn deeper and further into Greek politics, by virtue of the fact that any time there was to be any kind of dispute of conflict, the defeated party would seek help from Rome. While Macedon was generally amenable to being an ally of Rome, they did nevertheless maintain their independence.

In the year 179 BC, Philip V died and his son Perseus succeeded him. Perseus, much like all of the many Macedonian rulers before him, wished to unite all Greek-speaking peoples and territories under one rule, the rule of Macedon. Unfortunately for Perseus, Macedon by this stage in history was far too weak and diminished to attain this goal. Nevertheless, an ally to Rome, Eumenes II of Pergamum, led Rome to believe that Perseus and Macedonia was a dire threat to Rome and that they would be wise to act or face destruction.

As a result of this pattern of rumor-mongering on the part of Eumenes II of Pergamum, in the year 171 BC, the great city of Rome declared all-out war on Macedon. In a bid for an advantage against what it had been lead to believe were vastly superior numbers, Rome rallied one hundred thousand troops and mobilized them into Greece. As it turned out, this massive Roman army was far larger than Perseus could have ever hoped to beat, and the rest of the neighboring cities and city-states were unwilling or unable to rally to their aid.

Rome was not yet the military juggernaut that it would become at its height under such men as Julius Caesar, Pompey the Great and others. As such, their generals at this time were prone to mistakes and miscalculations, and this siege was no exception. On account of this sub-standard leadership on the part of the Romans, Perseus and his forces were able to weather the siege for three years. In the year 168 BC, however, the Romans grew tired of the siege and sent the noted general Lucius Aemilius Paullus into Greece, where he took Macedon to task and dealt them a devastating and sound defeat at the first Battle of Pydna.

As a result of this crushing defeat, the Romans were able to capture Perseus, after which they took him to Rome. As a punitive measure, Rome then split up the kingdom of Macedonia into four individual and distinct states. At the same time, any and all Greek cities or city-states that Rome perceived to have aided or assisted the Macedonian kingdom, even in a passive way, were harshly punished as a means to deter future rebellions. Even two of Rome's allies, Pergamum and Rhodes, were punished and essentially lost their independence at this time.

Some years later, in the year 149 BC, a traveling adventurer, claiming to be the son of Perseus, lead Macedon into a rebellion in opposition to Roman rule. However, this was a clumsy and foolhardy endeavor, and the short-lived rebellion was crushed thoroughly. As a result of this failed effort, Macedon was annexed directly and became relegated to a subservient role as a Roman province.

With Rome now motivated and spurred on to crush and suppress any potential uprising or threat to its dominance, it moved to deliver the final blow to Greek independence. Rome demanded the surrender and dissolution of the Achaean League, which was the last true body of Greek independence and strength. Unsurprisingly, the Achaean League decline to dissolve themselves, and formally declared war on Rome, feeling that if they were going to be destroyed and subjugated, they would prefer to fight and die. The majority of the Greek cities chose to aid and assist the Achaean League and rallied in their support. Stories tell us of even slaves be freed en masse in order to fight for an independent Greece. The Roman consul at this time, Lucius Mummius, brought his army from Macedonia and advanced on Greece, defeating them at Corinth. He and his army then razed the Greek city to the ground.

Finally, in the year 88 BC, the King of Pontus, Mithridates the Great, was the last Greek ruler to rebel against Rome in the Ancient era. He raised an army and rode across Asia Minor, slaughtering upwards of one hundred thousand Romans as well as the allies of Rome. Even though Mithridates was himself not Greek, several Greek cities nevertheless rallied around him, including Athens, and they revolted and overthrew their leaders, who were puppets that had been installed by Rome.

Later, however, Mithridates the Great was once and for all driven away from Greece by the famed general Lucius Cornelius Sulla of Rome. After which, the vengeance of Rome once again befell the Greek world. Mithridates the Great was himself was not finally defeated until the year 65 BC, in which he was at last defeated in battle by one of the most prominent generals of the Late Roman Republic, Gnaeus Pompeius

Magnus, who was also known as Pompey the Great.

Later on, Greece saw further ruin and destruction at the hands of Rome during the Roman civil wars, some of the battle of which took place in Greek territories. At last, in the year 27 BC, the first emperor of the newly formed Roman Empire, Augustus annexed Greece directly to the Roman Empire and gave them the name the province of Achaea. Much of the lands and territories of Greece were demoralized and depopulated by this point, on account of their struggles and conflicts with Rome. However, several cities, such as Corinth and Thessaloniki, and Athens were able to recover their prosperity and relative status after not too long, on account of the Pax Romana, the period of peace that came with the consolidation of power by the Roman Empire.

Chapter 5: Roman Greece

The Roman era of Ancient Greece refers to the period when the Roman Republic dominated the region, and eventually the Byzantine Empire. Collectively, these structures of Roman governance are referred to as the Roman era.

Ancient Greece under Roman rule began with the Corinthian's defeat against Rome in the Battle of Corinth, which took place in the year 146 BC. While that victory was indeed the beginning of the Roman supremacy of the Greeks, Rome did not definitely occupy the Greek world until the Battle of Actium, which took place in the year 31 BC. This was the great, historic battle in which the man who would become the first emperor of the new Roman Republic, Augustus, defeated his Greek foes, the Ptolemaic Greek Queen Cleopatra VII, and her general and lover, Mark Antony. The following year, Augustus proceeded to take over Alexandria, which at the time was the last true center of Hellenistic Greek culture.

The Greek world stayed under Roman rule for hundreds of years, all the up until the year 330 AD, when the great Empire of Rome went on to adopt the city of Byzantium as Nova Roma, the new capital of the Roman Empire. At this stage in history and afterward, the Eastern Roman Empire shifted into a mostly Greek-speaking territory.

Early Roman History

The geological feature described as the Greek peninsula first fell to Roman rule in the year 146 BC. This change in rulership was the result of the Battle of Corinth. The Battle of Corinth was the major conflict between Rome and Macedonia in which Rome was victorious and Macedonia became a province of Rome after it was directly annexed by the Roman republic. At this same time, on account of a newly bred mistrust for the Greek land and territories, Macedonia's new Roman appointed prefect carefully and cautiously surveilled the rest of southern Greece.

Some of the more cunning and willful of the Greek poleis were able to generally avoid taxes, and largely maintain some degree of at least partial independence. In the year 133 BC, the King Attalus III passed away. This was significant for two reasons. The reason it was significant is on account of the fact that he was the ruler of the Kingdom of Pergamon, which at this time was relatively independent of Roman rule, although it was heavily pressured by Rome and very much under Roman influence. The second reason as to the significance of King Attalus II's passing of the Kingdom of Pergamon was because in his final will and testament, he had left his kingdom and his territories to the people of Rome. This act resulted in the Kingdom of Pergamon effectively being incorporated into the Roman territories.

But while this convenient bequest was a boon for Rome, they were not quick to secure their claim over their new territories. During this time a pretender to the throne of the kingdom of Pergamon, going by the name of Aristonicus, rallied a revolution with the assistance of the stoic philosopher and revolutionary Blossius.

That uprising was expectedly put down in the year 129 BC, at which point the former kingdom of Pergamon was dissolved and its territories were divided and shared between Rome, Cappadocia, and Pontus. Later on, in the year 88 BC, Athens revolted with the aid and assistance of several other Greek cities. That popular uprising was also quickly and relatively easily crushed by the highly effective and celebrated Roman general Sulla.

A few decades later, as the Roman Republic collapsed under its own weight and descended into civil war, the lands and territories suffered even further, as the wars and conflicts of Rome continued to devastate the land. Finally, in the year 27 BC, the brand new emperor of the newly-minted Roman Republic consolidated the entire Greek peninsula and organized it as a province under the name of Achaea.

The lands and cities of Greece were absolutely devastated economically by these turbulent and disruptive events. However, after the Roman civil wars came to an end, the economies of these cities and lands began to rise back up dramatically. The Greek cities that were located in the region of Asia Minor generally recovered in earlier and faster than the cities and lands of the Greek peninsula proper. This was very likely on account of the fact that the cities located on the peninsula had seen more and heavier damage by General Sulla's Roman forces, then had the cities throughout the lands of Asia Minor.

But in the years that followed, the Romans sunk some very heavy investment funds into these cities for the purpose of rebuilding them and getting them into a state of growth and prosperity once again. For the newly declared province of Achaea, the city of Corinth was decided on to be the new capital city. And while Athens was not as politically or militarily dominant as it once had been, it went on to see continued prosperity as a hub of learning and philosophy throughout the Greek, and now Roman, world.

The Early Roman Empire

Under the rule of the new Roman Empire, the life of most people in the lands of the Greek world continue more or less the way it had previously, only under a different rule and with different leaders. But by and large, the culture of Rome was more likely to be influenced by Greece, than for Greek culture to be influenced by Rome. Much of the culture and beliefs of

Rome during this time were in fact very highly influenced by the culture and lives of the Greek people. Much of the Roman Empire arts and literature were also inspired and otherwise influenced by the arts and literature of Greece both contemporary and historical. One particularly notable example of such cultural borrowing by means of arts and literature is that of the *Aeneid* of Virgil, which was noticeably inspired by the epic works of the Greek poet Homer. Similarly, many works of Roman writing during this time were indeed written in imitation of the Greek style by their Roman authors, such as, for example, the works of the author and philosopher Seneca the younger.

While it is certainly true that not all Roman nobles valued the Greeks or Greek culture, many of them looked down on the Greek people as being backward or uncivilized. At the same time, a great many of the Roman nobles, many of them went on to quite an enormous deal of fame and fortune, duly embraced the philosophies and literature of the Greeks. The Greek language went on to become the primary language of the elite and the highly educated in Rome. One important and particularly notable example of this Roman embrace of the Greek language and culture was that of the great general Scipio Africanus, who is considered to be one of, if not singularly the greatest military commander, tactician and strategist to have ever lived, often being mentioned in the same sentences as Alexander the Great, Julius Caesar and Napoleon Bonaparte.

Scipio Africanus studied a great deal of philosophy, and he considered the culture and science of the Greeks to be an example that should be followed.

After a similar fashion, most of the emperors who ruled over the duration of the Roman Empire tended to admire and respect Greek culture and generally all things that had a Greek origin or a Greek nature. An excellent example of one such Roman emperor with a strong passion for Greek culture was that of Roman Emperor Nero. In the year 66 AD, the Roman Emperor Nero went to Greece for a visit and for the Ancient Olympic Games. Emperor Nero, to everyone's surprise, actually performed in the games, despite that fact the rules for the Ancient Olympic Games prohibited anyone who was not Greek from participation. The Greeks honored him by proclaiming him the victor in every contest. Emperor Nero returned the honor in the year that followed, at the Isthmian Games in Corinth, where he proclaimed the freedom of all Greeks, just as had done Flamininus some two hundred years prior to this. It has also been noted that the emperor Hadrian was rather quite fond of the Greeks and of their culture. He commissioned the building of the arch that bears his name, the Arch of Hadrian in Athens, which happens to be the city where he served as an eponymous archon prior to becoming the Emperor of the Roman Empire.

As a matter of fact, many of the public buildings and temples that were built in the Greek cities during this period were specifically commissioned by the emperors and the wealthy class of elite Roman nobility. This fact is particularly true of the city of Athens. In fact, one of the more famous buildings in Athens, the Roman Agora, was commissioned by Julius Caesar himself, although it wasn't completed until after his death, by Augustus. The primary gate of this structure, the Gate of Athena Archegetis, was dedicated to Athena, the patron goddess of Athens. In the center of this freshly built Roman Agora was built the Agrippina, by Marcus Vipsanius Agrippa.

In the year 50 BC, Andronicus of Cyrrhus built the Tower of the Winds, however, it is possible that this structure may actually predate the Roman portion of Athens in its entirety. In a very similar fashion, the Roman emperor Hadrian was also a very strong admirer of the Greeks and of Greek culture. It is suggested that he even considered himself to be an heir to Pericles, and as such he as well made numerous contributions to the city of Athens.

One of these numerous contributions made to Athens by Hadrian was the Library of Hadrian. Another particularly notable contribution and accomplishment on the part of emperor Hadrian to Athens was his completion of the Temple of Olympian Zeus, a temple so massive and imposing that construction on it had begun some six hundred and thirty-eight years before its completion by the tyrants of Athens during the Age of the Tyrants in the Archaic era of Ancient Greece. At that time, the construction of the Temple had been abandoned as it was believed that to attempt the construction of a building on such an enormous scale would appear to be hubristic before the gods.

After the construction of this remarkable Temple of Olympian Zeus was completed, the people of Athens showed their gratitude to the emperor who contributed so much to their city by commissioning the construction of the Arch of Hadrian in honor of the emperor Hadrian. Leading away from the Arch of Hadrian, in the direction of the Roman Agora, to this day exists Hadrian Street.

With the establishment of the Roman Empire, a period of comparative stability and peace followed in its wake. This time period is referred to as the Pax Romana. In the entire course of Greek history up until that point, the Pax Romana represented the longest period of peace Greece had ever seen. During this period, Greece also became an essential crossroads for the trade network by land and sea between the city of Rome itself, and the eastern territories of the Roman Empire, which were still largely Greek-speaking by this point in time. The language of Greece too was still highly crucial to the success of the Roman Empire, as it became not only the primary trade language and bridge language for the Empire, but the Greek language was also taken up by Roman elites. To complete this pattern of cultural exchange, even many Greek scholars and intellectuals did much if not most of their work within the city of Rome.

In the earliest decades of the Roman Empire and of the Roman Empire's rule over Greece, Early Christianity grew stronger and more powerful throughout both the Greek world and throughout the entire Roman Empire. Saul of Tarsus, who was more well-known by his Christian as the Apostle Paul, made several preaching campaigns around the Mediterranean, including Athens, Corinth, and Philippi. Before long, the Greek world became more Christianized than almost any other part of the entire Roman Empire.

Late Roman Empire

Later on in the history of the Greek and Roman worlds, namely, during the second and third centuries AD, Greece had been divided into several distinct provinces, including Macedonia, Achaea, Thrace, and Epirus. During the last years of the third century AD, as part of the reign of Diocletian, Moesia came to be organized into a diocese, which was under the rule of Galerius. Under the rule of Emperor Constantine, the first Roman Emperor to convert to Christianity, and then declare Rome to be a Christian Empire, Greece came to be governed under the prefectures of Thrace and Macedonia. Later, Roman Emperor Theodosius further split up the prefecture in Macedon into six smaller provinces. These were Macedonia, Epirus Nova, Epirus Vetus, Thessalia, Achaea and finally Creta. Meanwhile, the Aegean islands made up the province of Insulae, which was part of the Diocese of Asia.

During the period of history which corresponds to the reign of Romulus Augustulus, Greece was forced to face down several different invasions, perpetrated by the Vandals, the Goths, and Heruli. In the later period of the fourth century AD, a man named Stilicho, assumed the role of ruler of the land on behalf of the real ruler Arcadius, under false and duplicitous pretenses. He was a general of the Roman army who was of a particularly notably high rank. But while he was half Vandal, he was married to the young woman who happened to be the niece of Emperor Theodosius I, and as such was able to secure for himself a high degree of respect and responsibility within the Roman army. But while this was most certainly a high water mark in terms of the advancement of members from within the Germanic or, Barbaric tribes, within the Roman army's command structure, Stilicho made the unpopular decision to evacuate Thessaly when the Visigoths invaded.

The Chief advisor for Arcadius, a man by the name of Eutropius, made a concession by allowing Alaric, the man who crowned himself the first King of the Visigoths, between the years of 395 AD and 410 Ad, to enter into Greek territory. In so doing, Alaric ransacked the lands of Greece and went through the territory, looting cities. One by one, cities fell throughout the lands of Ancient Greece. The city of Athens was looted. The city of Corinth was also thoroughly looted during this brutal campaign. And as well, the lands of the Peloponnese, already having been ruined by war and hardship for hundreds of years, was also entered, pillaged and looted for all it was worth.

The pretended named Stilicho was eventually able to mount a counter-offensive and pressed his men into service for the express purpose of removing King Alaric of the Visigoths out of Greece altogether. Eventually, in and around the year 397 AD, Stilicho was indeed able to drive Alaric out of Greece. Whether this whole episode was just the natural course of events, or whether it was some kind of elaborate ruse by the invading barbarians is unclear to this day, and was likely even less clear at the time, as these events were marked by secrecy, silence and cunning, but nevertheless, Alaric was named magister *militum* in the land of Illyricum. The position of magister *militum* was a very high levers military command post that was used prominently in the late Roman Empire, thought to have begun being implemented around the time of the Roman Emperor Constantine. Later though, after a short amount of time with Alaric using his position of magister *militum* for whatever purpose he may have taken it, he and the rest of the Goths moved on and migrated west toward Italy.

On the way, they managed to sack the great city of Rome. This monumental event in history happened in the year 410 AD. Later, as they continued to move west, they moved into the Iberian Peninsula and were able to build up the Visigothic Kingdom. This brand new kingdom made up of what the Romans considered to be barbarians ended up enduring for hundreds of years and lasted all the way until sometime in the year 711 AD when the Arabs arrived and were able to wrest control from the Visigoths.

The eastern half of the now divided Roman Empire commonly referred to as the Eastern Roman Empire, or the Byzantine Empire continued on with Greece remaining an important part of this relatively unified half of the Roman Empire in the east. While it was believed by historians for a long time that the Greek world suffered greatly during this time, it is now believed that the Greek peninsula was actually more likely to be rather prosperous during this time. In fact, it is likely that it was one of the most prosperous regions in all of the lands of the Roman Empire. More recent archaeological research has revealed that the polis system of city governance and wealth generation were still active and prosperous quite possibly all the way up to and into the sixth century AD.

We have even recovered contemporary texts written during this time, such as for example the *Syndekmos* of Hierokles, which show us that Greece during the late Antiquity was in fact very highly urbanized and had within its borders somewhere in the neighborhood of 80 cities. Today, in our modern era, the idea of Greece being extremely prosperous during late Antiquity is much more widely accepted. It is now believed that during in between the centuries of the fourth and seventh centuries AD, it is quite likely that Greece was one of the most economically successful regions of the Mediterranean in the east.

Chapter 6: The Byzantine Empire and the Greek Legacy

The lands of Greece and the entire Greek world had been under Roman rule for centuries now. As the Roman Empire itself began to fracture and weaken, tumultuous times would come with it. Eventually, the Roman Empire was split into two distinct empires, the Western Roman Empire and the Eastern Roman Empire. The Eastern Roman Empire would also be referred to as the Byzantine Empire.

Invasions and Changing Times

The lands of Greece fell within the boundaries of the Byzantine Empire. During the changing and shifting times of the early centuries of the Common Era, Greece largely changed and shifted with the times alongside the massive and still very powerful Byzantine Empire.

After Antioch and Alexandria fell to the Arabs, Thessaloniki became the second largest city in the Byzantine Empire, second only to Constantinople. Thessaloniki would then be declared the 'co-regent' alongside Constantinople. At this time, the

Greek peninsula continued to be one of the biggest and strongest hubs of Christianity throughout the entire late Roman and well into the early Byzantine periods.

After having recovered from a number of invasions perpetrated by the Slavic peoples, the wealth of the Greek world was restored. Later on, as the Byzantine era progressed, certain events began to change the way the Byzantine Empire operated. Such notable events include the defeat and occupation of Constantinople by the Latin Empire of Romania, as well the invasion of Asia Minor by the Turko-Persian Seljuk Empire. These particular events, along with many others, led the Byzantine Empire to turn its focus and interests toward the Greek peninsula. Despite this period of domination by the Latins to the recovery of the Byzantine Empire and all the way through the final fall of the Byzantine Empire to the Ottomans, the Peloponnese remained prosperous economically, although many others Greek cities were rather successful all through these changing eras as well.

By the time of the reign of the emperor Andronicus III Palaeologus, who took power over the Byzantine Empire in the year 1328 AD, the Byzantine Empire still had secure control over the majority of Greece. By this time the urban metropolis center of Thessalonians was of particular importance, and the Byzantine Empire controlled this region, but not a whole lot else. The land of Epirus was technically under Byzantine rule, but would still take any opportunity it could find to rebel, although it was finally recovered for good in the year 1339 AD.

Much like it had for hundreds of years, the lands of Greece were largely used as a battleground. It saw a large degree of the fighting during the civil war which occurred in the 1340s between John VI Cantacuzenus and John V Palaeologus. Meanwhile, at more or less the same period in time, the Ottomans and the Serbs began to attack the Greek lands.

Disease

The lands of the Peloponnese, which during this period of time became primarily known as the Morea, was, by and large, the epicenter of the Byzantine Empire and was definitely the most fertile and productive region. The cities of Monemvasia and Mystras were also rather prosperous and populous, although the Black Plague did a number on them in the middle of the 14th century. They were able to recover and remain successful and prosperous, however. During this time, Mystras even rivaled the great capital of Constantinople for a time in its importance. In this era, many emperors sought to unite the Empire with the Roman Catholic Church, which had gained incredible power and influence by this time, but the Greek lands were still a great stronghold for the Greek Orthodoxy, and they persistently and bitterly fought against these attempts, despite the fact that aligning with the Roman

Catholic Church would have opened up the empire to assist from the west against the Ottoman Empire.

By this point in time, the Ottomans had begun their assault and conquest of the lands of Greece as well as the Balkans, which persisted and continued throughout the latter part of the 14th century AD and the earlier years of the 15th century AD. The future emperor Constantine XI, who at the time was a despotic ruler of the city of Mystras, managed to recapture the city of Thessaly from Ottoman occupation in the year 1445, although even with this victory, there was little that could be done in order to capture or reclaim the rest of the Ottoman territories. In the year 1453 AD, the Ottomans were finally able to capture the city of Constantinople, and with it, they captured and killed Emperor Constantine.

Constantine's death marked the fall of Constantinople. By the year 1458 AD, the Ottomans had also managed to capture the Aegean islands as well as the city of Athens. However, the Ottomans did leave a Byzantine despotate to rule the Peloponnese until the year 1460 AD. At this time, the Venetians still maintained control of the island of Crete as well as some Greek ports, but apart from that, the Ottomans were in control of many regions of Greece. However, the mountains and regions with heavy forestation remain free and under Greek control.

Final Thoughts

Thus, we come to an end of the 2000-year Greek saga that began all the way back in early antiquity by a civilization of people clawing their way out of a dark age. A people that would go on to build the foundation of democracy, art, science, and culture that persists well into this day, and has lasted through many, many empires, great and small. It has stood the test of time, and now to this day, the lands of the Greek nation and the historic locations and sights of this historically and cultural priceless land stand there for all who wish to take heed and notice. There is always much to be learned about history, and finding out about our ancestors will always play a vital role in our modern world.

Conclusion

You've made it through to the end of *Ancient Greece*! Let's hope it was informative and able to equip you with the knowledge and tools you need to.

The next step is to keep learning what you can about the Ancient World. Learning about history is one of the most important ways to gain insight into the world around us, and gives us an important lens through which to view our modern world. What's more, awareness of the mistakes and advances of the past will better equip us and our society for a better future.

In this book, we learned much about Greece in antiquity. We learned about the early rise to power of the Archaic Greek world as it rose out of the ashes of the old Mycenaean kingdom. We then dove into Classical Greece and the major developments that were made in the fields of politics, the arts as well as the military tactics and strategies that have made a massive impact on the world. The principles and concepts within these fields are still used both during contemporary times and equally, down to our today.

Moving past the classical period, we learned about the era of Hellenistic Greece when the makeup of the Greek world changed dramatically and spread throughout the then known world. Also, we learned about the rise of the City-States, such as Athens and Sparta, which would go on to be dominated by Macedon.

Finally, we dug deep into Greece under Roman rule, and how it went on to take its place in history as a land of cultural heritage that would have a significant and enduring legacy.

If you found this book useful in any way, a review is always appreciated!